Your Amazing Itty Bitty® Getting Financially Organized Trilogy

Three Itty Bitty Books Combined to Organize Your Financial Life

Marie Burns, CFP®
Certified Financial Planner

Published by Itty Bitty® Publishing
A subsidiary of S & P Productions, Inc.

Printed in the United States of America

Itty Bitty® Publishing
311 Main Street, Suite D
El Segundo, CA 90245
(310) 640-8885

ISBN: 978-1-950326-63-1

This booklet is intended to be informational only and is not intended to be construed as tax or legal advice. Readers should consult their own tax and legal advisors who are familiar with their personal situation.

Three Amazing Itty Bitty® Financial Organization Books

Three books in one: Steps to Organizing Your Finances

Most of us would agree that the last thing we want is to be a burden to anyone. Our first worry is the money aspect of that, not being able to afford or provide financially for any needs we may have prior to our passing.

But often the most time consuming and stressful aspect for family can be the estate settling process itself which can last three months to three years. Why put them through that stress?

All the steps you need are in these three Itty Bitty® Books—now compiled into one book:

- Your Amazing Itty Bitty® "Before" Death Financial Checklist
- Your Amazing Itty Bitty® "After" Death Financial Checklist
- Your Amazing Itty Bitty® Getting Financially Organized Book

Ensure a shorter, less stressful, and often less costly process for your family today.

Dedication

This book is dedicated to the women I have helped over the years who also inspired me to write this book.

Stop by our Itty Bitty® website to find interesting information regarding preparing financial checklists:

www.IttyBittyPublishing.com

Or visit **Marie Burns** at

www.mindmoneymotion.com

Table of Contents

Book 3 –Your Amazing Itty Bitty® Getting Financially Organized Book

Your Amazing Itty Bitty® "Before" Financial Checklist Book

15 Important Actions to Complete Before the Loss of a Loved One

Marie Burns, CFP®
Certified Financial Planner

Book 1 - Your Amazing Itty Bitty® "Before" Financial Checklist Book

Introduction

This Itty Bitty Book will guide you in completing 15 important actions that will help you update your financial records before you're gone, which will save:

- stress
- time
- money

and help preserve family relationships.

Remember the old joke: How do you eat an elephant? Answer: One bite at a time. This book breaks down the updating of your financial records into small "bites," so it doesn't feel so overwhelming and you are more likely to take action on implementing the necessary steps.

Being humans, we tend to procrastinate, especially when everything is going well. But during the calm (before the storm) is the best time to think clearly and act rationally to put your financial house in order.

Those who fail to plan, should plan to fail.

Step 1
Organize:
Get Your Ducks in a Row

The more you organize your records in advance, the easier it will be for others to deal with after you're gone. Categorize as much as you can in one location (use hanging files, binders, electronic files, whatever you prefer).

1. Designate major filing sections: banking, debt, employee benefits, estate planning, health, household, insurance, investments, miscellaneous, personal property, real estate, retirement income, school, taxes.
2. Within each major section, you may want a separate file for sub-categories. Also, pictures or a video of household items are helpful in the personal property section.
3. Once the files are created, sort and file or scan all documents or statements into the appropriate file.
4. After filing is complete, keep up with filing additional documents as you receive them.

Filing Section Sub-Category Examples:

- Debt: car loan, credit card, mortgage, student loan
- Health: dental, medical, vision
- Household: appliances, computer, furniture, phone
- Insurance: auto, home, life, long-term care, umbrella
- Investments: annuity, employer plan, IRA/Roth account, non-retirement account
- Personal property: boat, guns, jewelry, vehicle
- Real estate: primary home, second home, rental, land
- Retirement income: Military, Pension, Social Security (if you haven't already, go to ssa.gov to set up your username and password so you can download a current Social Security statement annually)

Step 2
Organize:
I Own, I Owe

Compile a list of everything you own and update it at least annually. Your goal is to summarize in one place the value of everything you own, as well as everything you owe (known as a Net Worth Statement).

1. Check online for examples of a Net Worth Statement format.
2. Date the Net Worth Statement and list all items or account names (referred to as assets) and their current market values, as well as balances owed (referred to as liabilities).

Tips for Compiling Your Net Worth Statement

- Make sure the account names listed match the company name shown at the top of the statements they reference. For example, if you have a Roth IRA statement from E-trade, list it on the Net Worth Statement as E-trade Roth IRA, followed by your name.
- Specify account ownership type in the account names whenever possible. For example, if you have a joint investment account at Fidelity, list it as a Joint Fidelity account on the Net Worth Statement.
- If applicable, you may want to itemize the contents of your safe deposit box at the bank and file that list in your banking file. Unless there are valuable items like jewelry, coins, etc., the safe deposit box items (often mainly documents) won't be listed on the Net Worth Statement.

Step 3
Organize:
The Magic Words

As kids, remember the magic word was always "please." These days the magic words are: your username and password. Having a password inventory has become a critical part of accessing family financial records, so you need to have a list of all your login information compiled for when you are no longer around:

1. Save your password list in one preferred place (document on your computer, app on your phone, password inventory booklet).
2. Keep passwords confidential and do not store them in an easily accessible or obvious location.
3. Update your password inventory each time you are forced to change your login information.

Password Inventory Tips

- List the website address, username and password for each entry.
- If there is a Notes section in your password inventory, you may want to cross-reference the name of the account(s) you are able to access for each entry.
- Include answers to security questions for each site, if applicable.
- Be sure appropriate family members know where to find this inventory when needed.

Step 4
Organize:
Who, What, When, Where, Why

Don't leave family members in the lurch when it comes to paying bills or notifying your creditors. Take the detective work out of it for them by maintaining a list of all common household expenses. Best to include the following details:

1. Who---name of company that gets paid
2. What---dollar amount to be paid
3. When---date expense is to be paid
4. Where---specify whether a check is mailed, the biller auto-deducts, or the payer manually pays online, etc.
5. Why---the service or product being provided

Wow, You Are Amazing!

By this point, you have already…

- Caught up on all your filing and organized your records into one location.
- Summarized in one list the assets you own and liabilities you owe (Net Worth Statement).
- Compiled a "cheat sheet" of the required login information for all of your accounts (Password Inventory).
- Collected all the necessary details in one spreadsheet or list of the common household bills.

You are on a roll and to be commended! Don't stop now…the organizing is almost done! One more step.

Step 5
Organize:
Inventory the "What Ifs"

The concept of having any insurance policy in place is to transfer the financial risk to an insurance company in case one of the dreaded "what ifs" in life occur (What if I die prematurely? What if I become disabled? What if I need long-term care?). Make a list of the insurance policies covering your risks.

1. Consider a bullet point list of policies that includes the company name, policy number, coverage amount and company/agent phone number.
2. Or you could use a spreadsheet format. Either way, specify the type of insurance.
3. An insurance folder containing just the declaration page from each policy (which captures most of the necessary detail) is another option to consolidate your insurance coverage in one place.

Your Insurance Policies

Common insurance policy categories:

- Accident
- Auto
- Disability (short- and long-term)
- Health/dental/vision
- Home
- Life
- Long-term care
- Umbrella liability

Don't forget the small policies like the $1,000 death benefit on some bank accounts or credit cards.

Organizing is done! Now on to the homework.

Step 6
Homework:
What's in a Name?

How you name/hold title to your assets, can significantly impact how they are treated after your death. Spending some time with your legal advisor to review the title of each asset on your Net Worth Statement, is an important discussion.

1. You need to decide where you want each asset or account to go after you are gone.
2. Then your legal advisor can help you advise the best way to title each asset so it gets there with the least cost and/or delay.
3. In general, a beneficiary designation on an account bypasses probate and allows that account or policy balance to go directly to the beneficiary.
4. An attorney licensed in your state of residence and who specializes in estate planning is the best resource for getting this advice because each state can have different laws.

Ways to Title Assets and Bypass the Additional Cost/Delay of Probate—THIS IS WHERE MOST PEOPLE FAIL!

- Joint with rights of survivorship ownership on non-retirement assets
- Payable on Death (POD) designation on bank accounts: savings, money market, CDs
- Transfer on Death (TOD) designation on non-retirement accounts: individual or jointly held stock, mutual fund, and/or bond accounts
- Transfer on Death (TOD) designation on a home, vehicle or property, also called a beneficiary deed
- Title the asset in the name of a trust
- Name primary and contingent beneficiaries on retirement accounts, annuities and life insurance policies (naming your estate as a beneficiary will NOT bypass probate)

Remember, a beneficiary designation is like a mini-will on each account. Each account will get distributed to the beneficiary on that account and it will never go to your will for distribution (unless your estate is listed as beneficiary but then it goes through probate first!), so keep beneficiary designations current and use Trust, TOD or POD in the account titling as recommended by your estate planning attorney.

Step 7
Homework:
The Legal Documents

The main reason to meet with a legal advisor is to draft or update your estate planning documents. The basic legal documents give instructions about what you want to happen with your assets after you are gone. They typically include a will and/or trust, Durable (Financial) Power of Attorney, and Health Care Power of Attorney.

1. Do you need a will or a trust? Estate Tax laws have changed over the years. Your wishes and desire/need for control must be factored into your legal advisor's recommendation on this question.
2. The Power of Attorney documents clarify who you want to make financial or health care decisions for you when you are alive but unable to act (if you are in a coma, for example).
3. Your agent for health care does not need to be the same person as your agent for financial power. Sometimes the one who you want to pay bills is not the same person you want to pull the plug!

Estate Planning Document Reminders

- When choosing your executor/personal representative/successor trustee, choose someone who is not only honest, but also organized with communication skills; a non-family member (fiduciary or corporate trustee) may make sense instead or jointly with a family member.
- Discuss whether your Durable (Financial) Power of Attorney should be immediate or "springing" (springs into action only at the time of incapacity). As we get older and/or for couples, immediate may be the best option but discuss with your attorney for the best advice regarding your situation.
- Review estate planning documents every 3-5 years, whenever there has been a law change, or when you have had a change in your circumstances.
- The best resource for this legal advice is an attorney who specializes in estate planning and is licensed in your state.
- Attorneys will remind you that you can write, date and sign a Disposition of Personal Property at any time to attach to your estate planning documents. This separate list itemizes things you specifically want to go to certain people (i.e. china to daughter, gun to son, piano to school, etc.)

Step 8
Homework:
The Morbid Details

Have you thought through or talked with family about your wishes related to organ donation? Burial vs. cremation? Service preferences? Writing down your desires related to final details saves family from guessing what you wanted.

1. Most states have a Final Disposition form or something similar so you can clarify your thoughts on burial vs. cremation, ceremony preference, organ donation, burial/ashes location, etc. in writing.
2. You may want to purchase a burial plot, tombstone, or mausoleum in advance to eliminate one more detail for family.
3. Some states or attorneys make a wallet card available to carry with you that identifies your health care agent.
4. Is there a desire to write an ethical will? An ethical will is like a legacy letter, a way to pass on your values, lessons you learned from life, or forgiveness of family or friends.

Final Celebration

Sometimes when an illness is involved, the terminal loved one may want to be involved in the final celebration planning, which could include:

- Selecting the location
- Planning the music
- Creating a menu
- Writing an obituary
- Leaving letters or making phone calls to loved ones
- Sharing memories, scriptures, photos, poems, quotes, advice
- Check out www.funerals.org for other planning considerations

Step 9
Homework:
To Each His Own

There may come a time when you need your Durable (Financial) Power of Attorney to act on your behalf while you are alive. Each financial institution will have its own paperwork requirement, so it's good to become familiar with what that entails in advance.

1. To be aware of the process and time frame that may be involved with needing your financial agent to act on your behalf, you may want to begin asking your bank, investment and retirement account providers what they require to name a financial power of attorney with them.
2. Each institution is likely to require their own form and will not just accept a copy of your Durable (Financial) Power of Attorney document.
3. Consider when you may want to initiate the financial power of attorney authorization process with each institution to avoid a delay at a more crucial time.

Incapacity

Before anything happens and a Durable (Financial) Power of Attorney authorization is needed, it is a good idea to make sure the person you named to make your decisions:

- is aware of your wishes and has a copy of the Durable Power of Attorney document
- knows where the original document is located
- has signature authority on a bank account
- if applicable, knows the location of, and has the ability to access, your safe deposit box and where the key is located

Consider travelling with a "To Go" bag that contains important information like a copy of your Power of Attorney documents, medication list, and ICE (In Case of Emergency) contact sheet.

Step 10
Homework: Who Gets What?

Remember that each beneficiary designation dictates the distribution of each account so make sure all of your beneficiary designations are current. Too often we list someone – then, life changes, people pass away, or relationships change, so your beneficiary designations may need to change too.

1. Consider naming primary and contingent beneficiaries on all accounts and policies. A contingent beneficiary specifies who would receive the account if both you and the primary beneficiary perished in a car accident together, for example.
2. We are usually aware of the need to designate beneficiaries on retirement accounts, life insurance policies and annuities but you should also confirm they are current.
3. You can name beneficiaries on non-retirement accounts, i.e. POD (Payable on Death) on bank accounts and TOD (Transfer on Death) on investment accounts and property.
4. Pets are not usually beneficiaries, but be sure you specify their needs and your wishes with family and in your will/trust.

Beneficiary Designations

- The best person to give you advice on naming beneficiaries is your legal advisor. He/she understands the big picture of your estate and knows what it is you are trying to accomplish.
- Discuss with your attorney the option to add "per stirpes" or "by rights of representation" wording (the ability to include grandchildren if their parents predecease you) to a beneficiary designation.

Too often, people misunderstand and believe that once their will or trust is drafted, that takes care of everything and that beneficiary designations don't matter because they have it all spelled out in their will or trust. But remember, a beneficiary designation acts like a little mini-will in dictating where each account gets distributed, so the account never references the will or trust for distribution instructions at all on most accounts unless the will or trust is listed as the beneficiary (and that may not be the best practice for tax reasons) or goes through probate because there was no beneficiary listed.

You need to consult your legal advisor for beneficiary designation recommendations – don't guess!

Step 11
Homework:
Monthly Moolah

When life suddenly changes, survivors or family members may need access to cash temporarily or need increased income for a short or long period of time. It's good to be aware of, or to consider putting some options in place in advance to address these potential income needs.

1. In the case of a couple, household Social Security income goes down after one passes away. The surviving spouse gets to continue receiving the higher of the two Social Security payments and the other payment stops.
2. Pension income often stops or is reduced after the death of the original recipient.
3. If you own a home, it may be wise to talk with your bank about setting up a HELOC (Home Equity Line of Credit) if not already in place, for immediate access to cash if/when needed.
4. Sometimes a reverse mortgage can be explored to leverage the value of a home as an ongoing income source (consult a tax advisor if looking into this option).

Social Security

As this program's rules evolve, these rules of thumb can change:

- For couples, it is often best for the higher income earner, if healthy, to delay taking the retirement benefit until as close to age 70 as possible to maximize the benefit for the surviving spouse down the road.
- If you live to your mid 80s or beyond, you will receive more lifetime income from Social Security if you delay taking your benefit until closer to or at age 70.
- Your Social Security benefit increases in value by 8% per year that you delay it, up to the age of 70 (so there is no benefit to waiting beyond age 70).
- Social Security was designed to provide about 1/3 of what a retiree may need to live on.
- Several factors should be considered with your financial advisor in determining the best claiming age: health, family longevity, other income sources, tax bracket now and later, Required Minimum Distributions, employment plans, survivor's situation and Roth conversion opportunities.

Step 12
Homework:
K.I.S.S.

The acronym K.I.S.S. stands for Keep It Super Simple (or Keep It Simple, Stupid!). Whatever you can do to simplify your financial situation in advance, will not only benefit you, but will mean less time and paperwork for your family later as well.

1. Consolidate your accounts. If you have more than one of the same type of account, ask yourself if that is necessary. It may make sense to combine similar types of accounts into one.
2. If you hold paper stock certificates, think about combining them in book entry form instead into a single account as this would mean less work for heirs down the road.
3. Close or consolidate small accounts.

Whew, The Homework is Done!

You should feel very proud of yourself for every step you have taken to get this far. Anything you have completed puts you in a better position than before you started and your family will thank you too.

- Life is full of surprises – not all of them are welcome.
- Working with licensed tax, legal and financial advisors is the smaller price to pay along the way than the costly mistakes, taxes, losses you or your family may experience without that advice.
- If incapacity or the end is near, there are a few more actions to consider…

Step 13
The End is Near:
The Tax Expert

No one wants to pay more taxes than required, at any time of life. There may be a few tax-saving opportunities that can be lost at death if not acted upon before death, so you should meet with your tax advisor to discuss as the laws do change.

1. Meet with your tax advisor to update him/her on the potential terminal or incapacity situation.
2. Inquire about whether there are any unrealized gains that should be realized in order to use up any tax loss carryovers from previous years that could otherwise be lost upon death.
3. Same question with charitable contribution carryovers that could be lost upon death.
4. Consult your tax advisor for any additional tax planning considerations allowable by current law.

Choosing a Tax Advisor

- Just like looking for a mechanic, hairdresser, dentist, etc., DO ask people you know who they work with and would recommend.
- Because you want to meet in person, DON'T call to set an introductory (complementary) appointment during the busiest times of the year (April 15, October 15 and year-end).
- Since you are looking for someone who works with people in your situation, DO ask for a description of their typical client.
- DON'T forget to provide copies of your last two years of tax returns in advance of the meeting in order to ask for a tax preparation fee estimate.

Step 14
The End is Near:
The Legal Expert

So many clichés in life end up being so true, including the one that reminds us "we get what we pay for." Don't try to take any shortcuts with your estate planning – see an attorney.

1. Ongoing visits with an estate planning attorney, especially near the end, will be invaluable in getting things where you want them to go with the least cost and delay.
2. Estate planning documents are less likely to be contested if drafted by an attorney vs. a fill-in-the-blank will/trust kit.
3. Gifting limits and charitable contributions can be thought through more thoroughly.
4. Direct payments to medical, dental or educational institutions (none of which count toward the annual gift exclusion amount) may make sense to consider.

Choosing an Estate Planning Attorney

- To find an estate planning attorney, get referrals from people you know.
- Meet with two or three attorneys (a complementary introductory meeting) who specialize in estate planning to understand the fees and get a gut check on how you might feel working with any of them.
- Ask for their thoughts about who needs a trust vs. a will and understand how they charge (flat fee or hourly).

Step 15
The End is Near:
The Planning Expert

The tax advisor helps consider taxes, the legal expert gives advice based on the law, but there is no one overseeing the big picture of your financial life with you so consider working with a financial advisor.

1. A CFP, Certified Financial Planner, has a fiduciary duty to advise on what is in your best interest.
2. For help acting on the tax and legal advisor's advice, as well as to consider all areas of financial planning, a CFP® can be your advocate and assist in communicating and implementing the advice of the team of advisors.
3. It's tough; we sometimes don't want our children too involved, this is not an area we are comfortable talking about in detail with other family or friends, so who else can we turn to?
4. You need someone licensed (so you are protected), experienced (so you are not the guinea pig) and trustworthy (so you don't get hurt), who will care about, and help to take care of your financial needs.

What a CFP® Can Help With

- Estate Planning---assisting with updating beneficiaries, account titling, and charitable/gifting based on the advice of your estate planning attorney and tax advisor.

- Education Planning---understanding and investing in college funding options.

- Income Planning---income and expense planning with prudent withdrawal strategies in conjunction with a tax advisor.

- Investment Planning---monitoring and advising on investing for growth and income in coordination with your tax advisor.

- Insurance Planning---analyzing options to address risks associated with death, long term care and disability.

- Retirement Planning---lifestyle planning to meet spending goals and needs in retirement to minimize the worry about running out of money.

Your Amazing Itty Bitty® "After" Financial Checklist

15 Important Actions to Complete After the Loss of a Loved One

Marie Burns, CFP®
Certified Financial Planner

Book 2 - Your Amazing Itty Bitty® "After" Financial Checklist Book

Introduction

This Itty Bitty® Book is designed to help you take action on some financial steps that are best completed

- within the first few days,
- after the first couple weeks,
- and over the next few months

after the loss of a loved one.

It is not uncommon, and it is very normal, to look back to the time shortly after someone's death and not remember saying or doing something that you know you did or were told that you did. When the brain is in trauma mode, it may "shut the door" to the logical side of the brain and camp out in the emotional side, unable to remember clearly for a period of time.

Having a process, documented notes, and an ordered action list can help you move forward with getting things updated while the brain is still recovering. Relying on the help of trusted family, friends and advisors is a must as well.

This Itty Bitty® Book will remind you not to make any major decisions, financially or otherwise, for 6-12 months after the loss of a loved one. In the meantime, you can take care of getting your financial house back in order by following the 15 steps in this book.

Step 1
The First Few Days:
Notify Family And Friends

Start a dated notebook now to log your activities. It's likely you will not remember many details for a period of time. Your first entry is who to notify about the death.

1. Doctor. A physician needs to be involved in declaring the date and time of death. If 911 has to be called, have in hand a do-not-resuscitate document if it exists. Without one, paramedics generally must start emergency procedures and, except where permitted to pronounce death, take the person to an emergency room for a doctor to make the declaration.
2. Family members. You may ask some family to help notify others.
3. Friends and neighbors. If the loved one was ill, he or she may have made a list of who should be contacted.
4. Clergy. You may need to set an appointment to discuss final celebration details as well.
5. Employer. Request any necessary paperwork when making this call.

Notifying Family And Friends Of A Death

Learning about the death of a loved one can be one of the most traumatic events in a person's life. Being the bearer of the news can be an incredibly emotional task and can wear many people out after only a few calls or visits, so consider options for spreading the word that a loved one has died recently:

- Phone Tree---Ask family members or close friends if they would mind making some calls
- Email---This can still be somewhat personal, yet you can reach a larger number of people at the same time. Make sure you've personally notified close family before you send a group email so no one is offended.
- Social Media---Lastly, after you've notified everyone that needs a personal contact, Facebook can be another way to notify friends so that they can get information about the memorial service. Facebook also has a Memorialization form online that can be used to delete a deceased person's account.

Step 2
The First Few Days:
Understand And Plan For Final Wishes

Hopefully, there is a Final Disposition form or something similar in writing that indicates your loved one's final wishes regarding cremation vs. burial, memorial preferences, etc.

1. Locate and review any estate planning documents that address final wishes (Health Care Directives, Final Disposition, etc.)
2. www.funerals.org can be a helpful resource regarding planning final services.
3. Order 10-20 certified copies of the death certificate (often available from the funeral home or county office). When dealing with paperwork later, you will need these certificates for most accounts and policies you have to deal with.
4. Place an obituary in relevant papers.
5. Make arrangements for someone to stay at the house during the service since obituary and funeral notices can alert burglars to empty homes.
6. Plan for all the details around the memorial service.

Things to Think About When Planning A Memorial Service

- Decide on an overall theme or main message that can be reflected in the music, decorations, location, etc.
- Pick a location that will accommodate and be convenient for the number of people attending.
- Think about a date that considers travel time for guests.
- Choose a person or people to lead the services.
- Determine whether flowers vs. donations or live plants vs. flowers will be preferred.
- Select and request readers/speakers and musicians.
- Gather photographs or other memorabilia to display.
- Address how memorial gifts should be provided.
- Ask for and accept offers to help with all of the above.

Step 3
The First Few Days: Call
The Appropriate Offices

Call the Social Security Office at 800-772-1213 to report a death (and the Veteran's Affairs Office or U.S. Office of Personnel Management (federal employee) if applicable).

1. Stop the deceased's deposits. The last deposit may need to be withdrawn if received after the date of death.
2. Claim the $255 death benefit if you are the surviving spouse.
3. Consider the option of applying for survivor benefits if you are an eligible surviving spouse and/or have minor children.
4. The Social Security Office will automatically notify Medicare, if applicable.

Social Security After A Death

- You cannot report a death or apply for survivor benefits online.
- There may be limits on how much you can earn while receiving benefits.
- Remarriage can affect survivor benefits.
- Pension income can impact survivor benefits.
- Your own retirement benefits should be considered when determining the best option for claiming survivor benefits.
- The Social Security Program rules may change over time, so it is best to make an appointment to meet with a representative at the Social Security Office to understand options and benefits.
- Discuss your options with your tax and financial advisors to maximize your income for the most tax efficiency **before** filing an election with the Social Security Office.

When applying for Social Security benefits, have available your spouse's birth and death certificates and your marriage certificate (if applicable), birth certificates of any dependent children, Social Security numbers, and copies of your spouse's most recent federal income tax return.

Step 4
The First Few Days:
Deal With The Emotional Brain

Emotions can seem to make a brain confused or think irrationally. Regardless of how the brain actually works, be aware that it is normal to have difficulty remembering things during this time, so write everything down.

1. Start and keep an ongoing notebook to document dates/times of all calls and the content of important conversations and meetings.
2. You may find it helpful to leave a separate notebook at the entrance of your home to log all visitors, deliveries, etc.
3. A helping hand can make a huge difference in easing the burden so delegate and accept assistance from those you trust.

Acknowledgment Cards After A Loss

Grief is devastating and exhausting in itself. After final services are over, the thought of handwriting an often large volume of notes for memorial cards or gifts, can feel overwhelming.

- Do you plan to send out cards? If so, who and how will you record and keep track of the gifts, names and addresses?
- Is there someone who can assist you with tracking and sending out the cards?
- Sometimes banks receive memorial gifts directly, but may not keep helpful records of the name and address of the donors – can that be prevented?
- If you decide not to send out cards, can you express gratitude instead with an acknowledgement placed near the cards/gifts, a note in the program, personal conversations, etc.?

There is no right or wrong decision on this. In a small community, an ad in the local paper may be appropriate. A short video memorial posted on Facebook with heartfelt words might be a solution. The main point is to think about it in advance so you can act on that decision without undue added stress at the appropriate time. Most especially, those who have experienced grief before will understand whatever you decide.

Step 5
The First Few Days:
Contact Your Estate Planning Attorney

You are not ready to have lengthy conversations right now, but call the estate planning attorney's office to set an appointment for 2-3 weeks out. Sometimes, this is the same attorney who drafted the will and/or trust documents.

1. Let the attorney's office know you are calling to make them aware of someone's passing and set an appointment to discuss further.
2. Ask to clarify which account should be used to pay for funeral and other short-term expenses.
3. They may share other specific information you should be aware of promptly.
4. Ask specifically what they would like you to bring to your upcoming meeting.

A Few General Things To Keep In Mind After Death

- No one should take or begin distributing anything until after the attorney meeting where roles and next steps can be clarified. It's wise to keep cash and valuables in locked locations.
- Keep lines of communication open so those involved understand the process and time involved; this can help avoid misinformation and suspicion.
- Set realistic expectations (for yourself and others); depending on the complexity of the assets involved, the process of finalizing the estate can take from three months to three years.
- Realize that almost everything that needs to be taken care of requires some paperwork to be signed, even when documents were prepared and updated correctly in advance, it is still a process that will take some time.

As an executor, there is fiduciary liability and exposure to you, personally, if you do not follow the terms of the will exactly. Seeking professional support from an estate planning attorney is a good idea.

Step 6
The First Couple Weeks:
Set Appointments With Your Advisors

It is important to get the estate overview
meeting with the attorney completed first (a
month or so after the death). Then you can
take what you learned from that meeting with
you to meet with the tax and financial
advisor. Set those appointments now so they
are on the calendar.

1. Start a file for all receipts and start an
   expense log to track bills paid after death.
   Take that with you to meet with the tax
   advisor, after meeting with the attorney.
2. Go to the bank to request date of death
   values on all accounts. You may need to
   go back again later after the attorney
   meeting to update account titles and
   beneficiaries at the bank as well.
3. If you are a surviving spouse, it is often a
   good idea to keep a joint checking
   account open until the estate settlement
   process is complete.
4. Call your financial advisor to request
   date of death values of all accounts in
   writing and to set up an appointment (for
   after you meet with the attorney).

Tips For Setting Appointments

- Use your log to write down the details: time, date, address of meeting, name of person you are meeting with, any directions as needed.
- Ask in advance what you should bring to the meeting and add those notes to your log.
- If there are specific concerns you have, let them know when you set the appointment about the agenda items that you want to be sure to have addressed.
- You may want to request a reminder call, email or text with the details of the appointment.
- Write your appointment down on a visible calendar as well as entering it into your phone and in your log.
- Plan to leave for your advisor meetings well in advance so you avoid feeling rushed and frazzled upon arrival; the agenda and circumstances are stressful enough.

Step 7
The First Couple Weeks:
Notify All Insurance Companies

Notify all insurance agents/companies to
determine if coverage needs to be adjusted,
terminated, or if benefits are to be paid out.

1. Hopefully there is already a list of all
    insurance providers, the policy numbers
    and contact information for you to call.
    Otherwise you will need to compile it.
2. Call each agent/company to notify them
    of the death and determine what is
    required to adjust, terminate or receive
    benefits from the policy.
3. When asked to provide a death
    certificate, clarify if it can be a copy or if
    it needs to be a certified death certificate.
    If certified, request that it be mailed back
    to you after processing to avoid having to
    order more later.
4. Keep notes in your log of the date, time
    and phone number you called, name of
    who you spoke to, information provided
    and next steps---in case you need to call
    again later.

Common Types Of Insurance That Should Be Notified

- Life
- Accident, if applicable
- Health/dental/vision
- Auto
- Home
- Long-term care
- Umbrella liability
- Disability (short- and long-term)

Don't forget the small policies, like the $1,000 death benefit typically offered on some bank accounts or credit cards.

Step 8
The First Month:
Inform Billers and Creditors

Notify billers (utilities, internet provider, cable company, etc.) and creditors (loan, mortgage and credit card providers) of death.

1. Make notes in your log of the details of each call.
2. Some payments may need to stop or be adjusted due to death.
3. Automatic payment details may need to be updated.
4. Accounts may need to be re-titled with new ownership or closed.
5. Inquire about whether any of the loans or credit card balances are automatically zeroed out in the event of death.
6. Notify all three credit reporting agencies and request a report on the deceased person. Make a note to contact them again several months down the road to request another copy of the reports in a new calendar year, to see if there has been any fraudulent activity after death.

Requesting A Free Annual Credit Report

You can request an annual free credit report from all three credit reporting agencies (Equifax, Experian and TransUnion) via any one of these three methods:

- Online at www.annualcreditreport.com
- By calling: (877) 322-8228
- By mail to: Annual Credit Report Request Service, P.O. Box 105281, Atlanta, GA 30348-5281

Step 9
The First Month:
Update Your Net Worth Statement

Before you see the attorney, tax advisor or financial advisor, you want to take the time to update your Net Worth Statement (current list of what you own and what you owe) so you can take it with you to those meetings.

1. Check out Net Worth Statement formats online, or use a yellow pad to list what you own on the left and what you owe on the right side.
2. Date the Net Worth Statement and list all personal property and account names (referred to as assets) and their current market values, as well as balances owed (referred to as liabilities).

Tips For Compiling Your Net Worth Statement

- Make sure the account names listed match the company name shown at the top of the statements they reference. For example, if you have a Roth IRA statement from E-trade, list it on the Net Worth Statement as E-trade Roth IRA, followed by your name.
- Specify account ownership type in the account names whenever possible. For example, if you have a joint investment account at Fidelity, list it as a Joint Fidelity account on the Net Worth Statement.
- If applicable, you may want to itemize the contents of your safe deposit box at the bank and file that list in your banking file. Unless there are items like jewelry, coins, etc., the safe deposit box items (often mainly documents) are often not listed on the Net Worth Statement.

Step 10
The First Month:
Meet With Your Estate Planning Attorney

Meet with your estate planning attorney during the first month to address the legal obligations of the personal representative and/or successor trustee, as well as to better understand the estate settling details and process.

1. If you do not have an estate planning attorney, find one through a referral from family, friends, co-workers or neighbors. It is helpful to work with someone recommended by a person you know.
2. Don't be tempted to ask family, a friend or a church member who happens to be a lawyer to draft documents or assist with the settlement process. If they do not specialize in estate planning as their primary practice, steer clear!
3. Every state has potentially different laws and probate can be different by county as well, so work with someone who's local, licensed and specializes in estate planning in your state.

Estate Settling Terminology To Ask Your Attorney About

- **Bequest**
  A gift of money or property given through a will.
- **Creditors**
  Individuals or businesses owed money by an estate.
- **Executor**
  Person named in a will to carry out its instructions. Female is executrix. Also called a personal representative.
- **Probate**
  The legal process of validating a will, paying debts, and distributing assets after death. Assets that go through probate usually include items you own in your name and those paid to your estate. In contrast, assets owned by a trust, or jointly with rights of survivorship, or payable-on-death or transfer-on-death, or insurance or other assets with beneficiary designations will not require probate. There are legal, executor, appraisal fees and court costs when an estate goes through probate. Probate fees are paid from assets in the estate before the assets are fully distributed to heirs.

Step 11
The First Month:
Miscellaneous "To Dos"

1. Go to the DMV (Department of Motor Vehicles) to cancel driver's license and transfer vehicle title.
2. Notify the Registrar of Voters.
3. Cancel any medication prescriptions, print subscriptions, and memberships.
4. Delete online personal accounts: email, social media, business sites, etc., to avoid fraud or identity theft. Procedures for each will vary.
5. Send out acknowledgments for cards, donations, etc., if you've decided that is something you want to do. This can also be delayed until a time that you are ready and able to tackle this project.
6. Contact the Post Office with forwarding information, if necessary.
7. Cancel all services no longer needed, i.e. phone, internet, cable, etc.

Getting Ready To Meet With Advisors

One of the most time-consuming financial aspects after someone has passed away is gathering all the documents that need to be assembled (unless they are organized in advance in a primary location).

- Death certificate(s)
- Will and/or trust
- Insurance policies (life, homeowners, health, disability, auto, etc.)
- Last credit card statements
- Investment account statements (IRAs, 401(k) plans, mutual funds, pensions, etc.)
- Last checking and savings account statements (including CDs and money-market accounts)
- Last mortgage statement
- Last two years' tax returns
- Marriage and birth certificates (of the deceased's spouse and children as well)
- An up-to-date credit report of the deceased

Step 12
The Next Few Months:
Sit Down With Your Tax Advisor

The IRS requires a final accounting after a death, and it's up to the executor or survivors to file the paperwork, so you need to see a tax advisor experienced in this area. Tax laws change, but in general, you need to discuss:

1. When a taxpayer dies, the taxpayer's estate may need to file a final return. Income will either be reported on the estate return, the return of the beneficiary who receives the income, or the tax payer's final return.
2. Money you inherit is generally not subject to income tax. Only interest earned from the time you become the owner is taxed.
3. A major exception to the general rule that inheritances are not subject to income tax is that money in traditional IRAs, employer-sponsored retirement plans (i.e. 401(k), 403(b), etc.) and annuities is taxed to the heir at the time of distribution, unless they are Roth IRAs.
4. There are many details involved (filing deadlines, cost basis, home sale rules, etc.) that must be considered and tax laws change. Talk to a tax expert for advice.

Working With A Tax Advisor

- Understand your filing status and deadlines. For the year in which the death occurs, the deceased's income taxes will be due on the normal filing date of the next year, unless extended. If you're the spouse of the deceased, you can still file a joint return for the year of death as long as you have not remarried.
- Ask about the differences in estate tax (federal and state), inheritance tax (only applicable in some states) and income tax, and their filing due dates.
- Discuss when disclaiming property as a beneficiary may be appropriate to consider.
- Bring your expense log and receipts with you to the meeting to help verify all deductions available.

Step 13
The Next Few Months:
Finalize Updated Documents With Your
Estate Planning Attorney

If you are a surviving spouse, update your estate planning documents with any new personal requests and get recommendations on new beneficiary designations.

1. You will likely need to continue meeting with the attorney for the ongoing estate settlement process, but also schedule a meeting to address updating your will/trust and power of attorney documents.
2. Your attorney will give you lots of options to think about (charitable, children/their spouses and grandchildren, gifting, etc.), so plan to take some time to digest that information and set another appointment to re-discuss before the attorney finalizes the updated documents.
3. You can always update your estate planning documents for a smaller fee (codicil of a will or amendment of a trust) later, so be aware that nothing you decide now is written in stone and can be changed again later.

Estate Planning Document Reminders

- Going forward, you should review estate planning documents every 3-5 years, whenever there has been a law change, or whenever you have had a change in your circumstances.
- The best resource for this legal advice is an attorney who specializes in estate planning and is licensed in your state of residence.
- Attorneys will remind you that you can write, date and sign a separate list (Disposition of Personal Property) at any time to attach to your estate planning documents. This list itemizes things you specifically want to go to certain people (i.e. china to daughter, gun to son, piano to school, etc.)

Step 14
The Next Few Months:
Re-evaluate Your Situation With A
Financial Advisor

The advisor who can help you after your meetings with the tax and legal advisors, plow through much of the paperwork with you, and make more sense of the big picture is a Certified Financial Planner, so make an appointment with one.

1. Reviewing income and expense needs are often your most immediate priorities. A financial plan is a comprehensive tool that can help address the short-term, as well as long-term income needs.
2. Immediate decisions regarding retirement account rollovers, annuity continuation or payout options, Social Security claims, life insurance proceeds, and required minimum distribution planning (if over age 70 ½) can all be analyzed for advice based on your situation.
3. Investment and insurance needs should be discussed.
4. Assistance with re-titling accounts and updating beneficiary designations will need to be completed together.

Working With A Financial Advisor

- Statistically, a majority of women leave the financial advisor they were working with when their spouse was alive within two years after death because they didn't feel connected or comfortable with that advisor.
- Check with those you know for recommendations (the tax and legal advisors can be a good referral source too) to someone who is not only knowledgeable and experienced, but also caring and trustworthy.
- Just like hiring anyone for their professional services, be sure you meet with two or three to understand their experience, investment philosophy, fee structure and approach to working with clients.

Step 15
Ongoing:
Take Care Of Yourself

No matter what your relationship was with the person you lost, those memories, along with the financial role you are now involved in, will require some healing. Remember to take care of yourself through this process.

1. Everyone is affected differently by stress and we all choose to de-stress in various ways as well. Make time for your preferred method (yoga, meditation, walking, prayer, etc.).
2. Reading articles or books about grief can help you understand some of your feelings better, as well as realize that what you are going through is normal.
3. Talk with family or those close to you about your thoughts and let them know if there are ways they can help. Allow yourself to grieve.
4. Joining a support group or working with a counselor (or both) could be something you might at least try for a period of time for your own healing.

Ideas That Have Helped Others Who Are Grieving

Something as basic as staying hydrated, eating well and getting enough sleep is very important. It's good for your general health and can help you think clearly through all the actions and decision-making you are involved in.

- Cry as often as you need to, it's an emotional release.
- Write, in whatever format helps you, a journal, poems, letters you may or may not send.
- Ask for help, perhaps with errands, grocery shopping, pet chores, meals.
- Breathe deeply, meditate, pray, or just sit quietly and take deep breaths.
- End each day with thoughts about what you are thankful for, keep a gratitude journal, notice the little things daily.

Your Amazing
Itty Bitty®
Getting Financially
Organized Book:

*15 Key Steps to Organizing Your
Financial Life*

Marie Burns, CFP®
Certified Financial Planner

Book 3 - Your Amazing Itty Bitty® Getting Financially Organized Checklist Book

Introduction

This Itty Bitty book will help you compile a summary and much of the detail regarding your current financial situation. This will assist you throughout your life to:

- Save you time whether it's paying bills, finding information, or doing taxes
- Keep your documents easily available and findable during an emergency
- Help eliminate missed opportunities
- Avoid penalties and/or missed payments

Additionally, people you care about will absolutely need to know this information if you become incapacitated or after you are gone. This book will provide a guide to:

- The content needed to capture your current financial snapshot in one convenient location.
- Help you think through and prepare so that your wishes are known and implemented as needed.
- Remind you to communicate with advisors and family about this topic.

Step 1
Organizing Your Paperwork

Getting and staying organized will be the foundation for making wise financial decisions because an overwhelmed or confused mind does not usually perform effectively. So use whatever system works best to organize and meet your needs and then stick with it.

1. Whatever format you choose to get organized (a binder, hanging files, a workbook, notebook, electronic files), keep your filing current and update it annually (around tax time or year-end is when you are receiving updated statements anyway).
2. Use a pencil if handwriting to make changes easily. Leave extra space or pages in case you need to add information later.
3. Give a copy to someone you trust or tell someone where to find it.

Congratulations for providing this gift to yourself AND those you care about!

Getting Organized

- You may want to compile a master list of where your various records can be found listing each item/category and its location.
- For storing original documents that will potentially be needed in the future, consider a fireproof safe at home or as a backup using a safe deposit box at a bank, though that may be sealed at death or unavailable in an emergency.
- If there are items you carry with you, i.e. credit card, driver's license, insurance card, etc., it is a good practice to make a copy of those items to store in your files as well and update those copies as they are replaced.
- Is there a duplicate set of keys (house, vehicle, etc.)? Where are they? Who else has a set? Is that information documented or easily found somewhere?

Step 2
Personal Information

Provide basic information about yourself as well as any significant others in your life:

1. Full name
2. Date of birth
3. Current address and contact information
4. Social Security number
5. Military details, if applicable
6. Church information, if applicable
7. Employer contact information

For a complete set of free forms to compile your personal financial inventory, visit The Financial Awareness Foundation at www.thefinancialawarenessfoundation.org

A few thoughts about passwords

Eventually, someone else may need to access your accounts when you are not available so keep up-to-date records in a secure place of your login information in whatever format you find most helpful (password booklet, password list, app on phone, file on the computer, etc.).

- Account name
- Website address
- Username
- Password
- Other information: security question/answer, where statements can be found if also in a file, phone number of account provider

Let someone you trust know the location of your password inventory via a note identifying its location in a fireproof safe, safe deposit box or sealed envelope to be opened by your trusted person when needed. This significantly reduces the risk of having your private information get into unwanted hands.

Step 3
Family/Other Information

Document details about immediate family, friends, and/or social groups.

1. Names (parents, siblings, children, friends, social group contacts, etc.)
2. Date of birth
3. Date and cause of death, if deceased
4. Current address and contact information
5. Family medical history
6. Marital status
7. Special notes

Including a copy of a family tree also can be helpful in clarifying relationships.

Special Notes

- If there are special circumstances or helpful things to understand about different people or various situations, a note of explanation can be helpful.
- Perhaps someone is typically only reachable on certain days or times, make a note.
- This may also be a section of the records where you want to include a list of important people to be contacted immediately in the event of your hospitalization or death.

Step 4
Advisors

Contact information of not only those who impact your financial health, but also your physical and spiritual health as well.

1. Attorney (estate planning, business, etc.)
2. Banker (personal, mortgage, business, etc.)
3. Insurance agents (home, auto, life, etc.)
4. Tax advisor
5. Financial advisor
6. Business partner
7. Doctor (family physician, specialist, etc.)
8. Clergy
9. Others

Contact information for Advisors

- Business name and website
- Individual name
- Physical address
- Phone number
- Email address
- Notes about availability, if known

Step 5
Income Sources

Document the details about your income sources:
1. Social Security
2. Pension
3. Military
4. Trust income
5. Earned income from an employer
6. Self-employment income
7. Alimony
8. Royalties
9. Dividend and interest income
10. IRA distributions
11. Other income sources

Don't forget to keep files and stay on top of your "hidden paycheck" too---your employer benefits:
1. Understand your benefits and their tax treatment
2. Keep your primary and secondary beneficiary selections current
3. Fully participate in your retirement plans and use other benefits wisely
4. Don't be tempted to overstock your net worth with company stock.

Tax returns will show additional data

Even though tax returns show annual income, it is helpful to itemize some detail for each income source in your record book or files:

- Approximate dates or time of year each payment is received
- Typical amount received
- Whether taxes have been withheld
- Survivor percentage, if applicable

Step 6
Expense Details

No one likes the word budget but try to itemize as much of the typical household "outflow" (aka budget) in some format i.e. spreadsheet, monthly calendar, itemized list, etc.

1. Include regular monthly expenses (utilities, phone, auto, etc.)
2. Make note of seasonal or non-monthly costs that get paid out i.e. semi-annual or quarterly insurance payments, property taxes, charitable commitments, etc.
3. Debt details i.e. mortgage, credit cards, auto loans, etc.

Common income/expense mistakes to avoid:

1. Spending more than you make
2. Incurring debt by over-spending
3. Not tracking your income and expenses
4. Impulse spending
5. Not having sufficient cash reserves

Why else does this matter?

- Even if you live in the same household with a spouse or significant other, it is very common that one of you regularly takes care of making sure that certain bills are paid and the other is not as involved. So for that person's sake, or think of the family member or friend who may need to step in and help with things if you are in the hospital for a time or to be the executor at some point, that individual has no idea what is paid, when, or why.
- These details can also be helpful in preventing fraud when someone has an idea of what should be going out of an account for legitimate reasons and be more watchful for items that are not on the expense list.
- If you haven't already gotten into the habit of requesting an annual credit report, please start now. In today's world of fraud and identity theft, reviewing your annual credit report can help you keep on top of any credit card abuse you may not be catching. Visit www.annualcreditreport.com

Step 7
Insurance Inventory

For each category of insurance, make sure the following information is available:

1. Type of insurance
2. Insurance company name
3. Policy number
4. Company contact information
5. Agent name and contact data
6. Ideally, the declaration page (single page summarizing the benefits of each policy) could be kept in a folder with the insurance inventory (and be easily accessible in the full insurance file as well)

Typical types of insurance

It can be helpful to make a list of all insurance types and then either fill in the details of each policy, write "see file" after each policy type or write in "NONE" after each policy type. That way it is clear that no one needs to guess about whether they need to look for a policy if it doesn't exist (life insurance or long-term care insurance, for example).

- Vehicle
- Rental
- Homeowners
- Property
- Earthquake / Flood
- Liability
- Personal Liability Umbrella
- Business
- Medical, dental, vision
- Life
- Disability
- Long term care
- Other

Step 8
Net Worth Statement

Your goal is to summarize in one place the value of everything you own, as well as everything you owe (known as a Net Worth Statement).

1. Check out the Net Worth Statement and Historical Net Worth templates available free from The Financial Awareness Foundation at www.TheFinancialAwarenessFoundation.org

2. Date the Net Worth Statement and list all items or account names (referred to as assets) and their current market values as well as balances owed (debt owed is referred to as a liability on a Net Worth Statement).

Tips for Compiling Your Net Worth Statement

- Make sure the account names listed match the company name shown at the top of the statements they reference. For example, if you have a Roth IRA statement from E-trade, list it on the Net Worth Statement as E-trade Roth IRA followed by your name.
- Specify account ownership type in the account name whenever possible. For example, if you are a couple and have a joint investment account at Fidelity list it as a Joint Fidelity account (or Trust Fidelity account if applicable) on the Net Worth Statement.
- If applicable, you may want to itemize the contents of your safe deposit box at the bank and file that list in your banking file. Unless there are items like jewelry, coins, etc., the safe deposit box items (often mainly documents) aren't often listed on the Net Worth Statement.
- Annually copy year-end statements for financial accounts and loans and keep them with your estate & gift plan documents.

Step 9
Cash and Investments

Your cash and non-retirement accounts list/file, often by account or institution, should include:

1. Owner of the account
2. Type of account
3. Name and address of institution
4. Account number
5. Contact information
6. Approximate balance (dated)
7. Name and address of any beneficiaries
8. Check out dozens of Know Where You Stand forms to itemize accounts, personal property, etc. available from The Financial Awareness Foundation free of charge at www.TheFinancialAwarenessFoundation.org

Typical types of cash and non-retirement accounts

- Checking
- Savings
- Money market
- Certificate of deposit (CD)
- Safe deposit box
- Stock certificates
- Individual bonds
- Individual, joint, TOD (Transfer on Death) or trust taxable investment accounts

Step 10
Retirement Accounts

List or have files for your tax deferred
(retirement) accounts showing:

1. Owner of account
2. Type of account
3. Name and address of institution
4. Account number
5. Contact information
6. Approximate balance (dated)
7. Name and address of any beneficiaries

Typical types of retirement accounts

Because each type of retirement account can have various tax or distribution rules, it is important to keep them listed/filed separately:

- Traditional IRA
- Rollover IRA
- Roth IRA (note the year first established)
- Employer plan (401(k), 403(b), 457, etc.)
- Qualified annuity
- Non-qualified annuity

Step 11
Real Property

Document properties you own and important details:

1. Ownership (i.e. individual, joint with rights of survivorship, trust, etc.)
2. Address of property
3. Approximate current market value
4. Purchase date and price
5. Notes about any additions to the property including dates and dollar value

Typical types of property

- Primary residence
- Vacation or second home
- Land
- Rental property
- Farmland
- Business property
- Cemetery plot
- Timeshare

Step 12
Personal Property

List or have in a file the general details about personal property owned:

1. Name of item
2. Purchase date
3. Purchase amount
4. Approximate current market value
5. A photo or video of household and/or valuable items can be very helpful for valuation, identification, and distribution purposes
6. Note if you are referencing this item in your will, trust, or in a Personal Property Disposition Letter of Instruction to your executor or trustee

Typical personal property items

- Antiques
- Art pieces
- Boat
- Collections
- Guns
- Heirloom items
- Home furnishings
- Intellectual property
- Jewelry
- Pets
- Season tickets
- Vehicles

Step 13
Estate & Gift Plan

In addition to having the actual documents stored in your file, safe, or safe deposit box, it is helpful to list the main people involved and their contact information:

1. Estate planning attorney
2. Executor/personal representative/trustee
3. Financial power of attorney and alternate
4. Health care agent and alternate
5. Beneficiaries named in your plan documents
6. Nonprofits named in your plan documents
7. Download the Estate and Gift Planning Location Sheet from The Financial Awareness Foundation at www.TheFinancialAwarenessFoundation .org
8. You may want to store your final wishes and information in a secure, central personal website. Check out www.Everplans.com as one option.

Typical estate planning documents

- Will
- Trust
- Health Care Power of Attorney
- Living Will, wishes for end-of-life medical care (often included in the Health Care Power of Attorney document)
- Durable (financial) Power of Attorney
- Final Wishes (funeral preferences)
- Disposition of Personal Property Letter of Instruction (a signed and dated list of personal property or sentimental items stating who you want to receive those items; you can write or re-write, sign and date this yourself at any time and store it with the will)
- Ethical Will (legacy notes to your family)

Step 14
Common Mistakes to Avoid

Once you have a clearer understanding of your financial picture, you are better positioned to understand some of life's biggest challenges. So in order to know where you stand, steer clear of these missteps:

1. Not regularly preparing, analyzing and updating a list of what you own and owe (net worth statement)
2. Not understanding what you own or owe
3. Increasing your debt due to overspending
4. Incurring high interest debt, especially debt that cannot be repaid immediately
5. Not keeping the title to your assets current with your estate and gift plans
6. Not keeping your beneficiary designations current
7. Not having a sufficient cash reserve and a back-up line of credit
8. Procrastination

Source: The Financial Awareness Foundation

Some general issues to think about once you're organized:

- Putting money aside for the future. Think about savings for shorter term needs and goals (like a vehicle purchase or home down payment) versus investments for longer term plans (like retirement).
- Saving for the "unexpected events" in life. Money magazine once reported that the average American experiences at least one "unexpected event" every 10 years. And those often involve the need for money, so be sure to have an emergency cash reserve built up (3-6 months of living expenses is a basic rule of thumb).
- Ignoring headlines as it relates to your long-term growth goals. Remember that in general, the media is focused on selling headlines not "boring" advice like the importance of diversification, rebalancing, and beating inflation.

Step 15
Miscellaneous

Once you have your financial house in order, consider the following tips:

1. Use automatic deposits and bank transfers to save time, postage, and missed bills as well as to pay yourself first (i.e. an automatic transfer to savings, a 401(K) contribution, an automatic Roth contribution, etc.).
2. Save time and money by reducing the number of payments you make for insurance premiums (i.e. annually vs monthly or quarterly).
3. To protect yourself from unexpected events, keep 6 -12 months of living expenses built up in a readily accessible cash reserve account.
4. As an additional safety net, establish a line of credit (based on the value of your home or a low interest rate credit card set aside for use only in emergencies) before you need it.

Other resources to check out:

You may prefer to use a fill-in-the-blank format to compile and maintain this information. There are several places you can find inventory templates:

- The Financial Awareness Foundation has compiled over 50 templates to get financially organized, available free of charge, at www.TheFinancialAwarenessFoundation.org
- www.whatifworkbook.com
- A book titled Get it Together by Melanie Cullen with Shae Irving
- A book titled The Household Financial Record Book by Chris T. Clark
- A book titled Your Family Records Organizer by Kiplinger
- A book titled Checklist for My Family by Sally Balch Hurme
- A book titled And Then There Was One by Charlotte Fox.
- www.MindMoneyMotion.com

Keep your financial house in order by annually reviewing and updating your checklists and your financial, estate and gift plans.

You've finished. Before you go…

Tweet/share that you finished this book.

Please star rate this book.

Reviews are solid gold to writers. Please take a few minutes to give us some itty bitty feedback.

ABOUT THE AUTHOR

Marie Burns started her career helping people balance their diet and exercise as a Registered Dietitian. A dozen years later, she began her journey as a Certified Financial Planner™ Professional and has been helping people balance their finances for almost two decades. Both roles involve guiding others to make behavior changes.

As the oldest of four children as well as the mother of four children, she is a natural fit for serving others as their "financial mother." Coming into the financial industry as a second career has helped Marie avoid the lingo of finance-speak and instead focus on translating complex subjects into understandable English.

When Marie realized that she was getting questions DAILY from friends, clients, and family related to helping aging parents, settling family estates, and couples worrying about how things will go when one of them is no longer around, she knew she needed to write a financial checklist.

Marie's goal is to create The Ripple Effect: these financial checklist books act like a rock launched into a pond and its ripples reach many more lives than she could ever positively impact in person. Marie writes and speaks to groups at www.MindMoneyMotion.com. She advises clients at www.FocusPointPlanning.com.

If you benefitted from this Amazing Itty Bitty Book you might also enjoy.

- **Your Amazing Itty Bitty Eldercare Book** – John Smith RN

- **Your Amazing Itty Bitty Alzheimers Book** – Dung Trinh, MD

- **Your Amazing Itty Bitty® Blissful Real Estate Investing Book** – Moneeka Sawyer

Or many other Itty Bity® Book available on line at www.ittybittypublishing.com

www.ingramcontent.com/pod-product-compliance
Lightning Source LLC
La Vergne TN
LVHW051248080426
835513LV00016B/1808